A Night in Brooklyn

A Night in Brooklyn

P O E M S

D. Nurkse

Alfred A. Knopf ⚞ New York 2012

THIS IS A BORZOI BOOK
PUBLISHED BY ALFRED A. KNOPF

Library of Congress Cataloging-in-Publication Data

Nurkse, D., 1949–

A night in Brooklyn : poems / by D. Nurkse.—1st ed.

p.   cm.

ISBN 978-0-307-95932-4

I. Title.

PS3564.U76N54   2012

811'.54—dc23   2011052655

Front-of-jacket photograph: "No. 39 Brooklyn,"
photograph by Lynn Saville, 2006 / Yancey Richardson Gallery

Jacket design by Carol Devine Carson

Manufactured in the United States of America

First Edition

For Beth, with love

Contents

PART ONE

A Night
in Brooklyn

Waking in Greenpoint in Late August

We wanted so much that there be a world
as we lay naked on our gray-striped mattress,
staring up at a trowel mark on the eggshell-blue ceiling
and waiting, waiting for twilight, darkness, dawn,
marriage, the child, the hoarse names of the city—
let there be a universe in which these lovers can wash
at the pearling spigot, and lick each other dry.

Making Shelves

In that lit window in Bushwick
halfway through the hardest winter
I cut plexiglass on a table saw,
coaxing the chalked taped pane
into the absence of the blade,
working to such fine tolerance
the kerf abolished the soft-lead line.
I felt your eyes play over me
but did not turn—dead people
were not allowed in those huge factories.
I bargained: when the bell rang
I would drink with you on Throop
under the El, quick pint of Night Train
but you said *no*. Blood jumped

from my little finger, power
snapped off, voices summoned me
by name, but I waved them back
and knelt to rule the next line.

Central Brooklyn

Behind the tenements lay wild gardens:
a swaddled fig tree, a muscat arbor.
I propped my forty-foot ladder against a shim
and climbed and began searing the high porches
with a butane torch. I gouged away dead bees,
resin, gum, soot from forges, caulk. Once
the lovers opened their blinds and watched
with pursed lips, hand in hand, her breasts
swaying slightly, his penis limp, their gaze
imperious and forgiving, and I missed a spot.
Then I painted white on white, when I finished
those streets were empty, no one lived there
except the rich, chalk-faced in their long divorce.

Flatlands

1

In that hotel, the mirror was naked.
I had never seen such a wavering cloud.
I ran my fingers along the glass.
It burned me slightly.

I didn't know who you are.
Just how to suffer, how to pass time,
and a few jokes whose appeal
was a forgotten punch line.

I poured you a cup of black wine.
It trembled. We could hear the trucks
roaring north and south—we were alone
in a huge city. August inched
sideways through the blinds.

2

I didn't know twilight would be naked.
The bells would be naked. Not knowing
would be naked.

3

We are told, only the moment is real,
all that exists exists in the moment,
but who knew how to get there?

We tried door after door
along those elm-lined streets
and heard just chimes
in triple-locked apartments.

Then we found it. It is here.
Though we are fading
all our actions last forever,
even fumbling at a button—

not in these words
but in the night sky hidden
at the center of the last period.

The Dead Remember Brooklyn

It is the great arguments
we are proud of, over a nibbled peach,
hair in the comb, a faulty lube job;
the reconciliations were always breathless
in borrowed rooms, sometimes in Queens
or Staten Island, we touched each other
shyly—we reminded each other
of loneliness and funk and beautiful pigeons
with oil-slick necks, cooing bitterly—
but there we lost each other,
in forgiveness; keeping score,
being wounded even in triumph,
walking home down leafy avenues
etched with the faint double line
of extinct trolleys, caressing
carved hearts under a sheen of sap
with a ragged nail, sleeping alone,
choosing the dream of betrayal,
entering by the wide door
and waking dead—there
we were superb. In Brooklyn
we held our own.

Red Antares in a Blue Mirror

On that close-nap futon
she taught me the difference
between being and becoming,
when she had finished
it was still twilight, a cricket
singing I, I, not furiously,
but with a cool insistence,
and I understood how the universe
was created—how it fit in a pinhead
fourteen billion years ago
when the first second lasted
almost forever, then it flew
in a trillion pieces and now
it obeys laws we recognize
the way a pet comes to look
like its owner: she was washing
at the cold tap, she was binding
back her copper hair, but I
had been given those absolute weapons:
suffering, abnegation, miracle:
and I had to use them
if only by counting, counting
until it was night and the rain
simmered in the dog's huge eyes.

The Dead Reveal Secrets of Brooklyn

We are frequently asked, *What is death like?*

Like tossing a Frisbee in Prospect Park,
making sure the release
is free of any twitch or spasm—
any trace of the body's vacillation—
willing the disc to glide forward
of its own momentum, never veering,
in a trance of straight lines.

Like waiting in traffic at Hoyt-Fulton
waving away the squeegee man
with his excessive grin and red-veined eyes.

Lying under your lover in Crown Heights
and divining a stranger's face
in the dark flash of her pupils.

Growing old in Kensington
on a block that reeks of dry cleaning
where you nod to three neighbors
and avoid the stare of a fourth
though a single brindle-tailed cat
patrols every dark garden.

Remember, death does not last,
not even a breath,
whereas the city goes on forever,
Cypress Hill, Gravesend, Bath Beach,
avenues screened by ginkgos,
vehemence of domino players
hunched over folding tables,

range on range of padlocked factories
that once made twine, hammers, tape
and now make small nameless articles
which we use to bind, shatter, or seal,
here where there is no self,
no other world, no Brooklyn.

Letter from Home

1

She writes: We would have voted against the war
but all the candidates opposed it.

We joined a march in dead of winter.
Weekend clerks gathered to applaud,
clapping to warm their numb hands.
In the tenements, hand-lettered signs supported us.

The soldiers said, *We will not fight,*
and the generals, *There is no cause.*
Whom would we invade? she writes:
we were the greatest power, perhaps of all time.
Then the war began in the corner of the eye.
At first it was mild and demanded nothing.
Now to want to die would be a privilege.
Now the invasion writes these words and can't stop.

2

They practice torture here, she says,
in the hospital, in the maze of corridors
color-coordinated for the insides of the body.
The laws allow it, but only as a last resort.
Only if the city might be destroyed otherwise.

3

We've created an external mind, she writes.
It has made our world small as a withheld breath.
If you want a weapon, you have only to imagine it.

4

Still a window blazes all night.
Still the cars pass.

Furnished Room on Pearl Street

As soon as we finished a section of the *Phoenix*
we wedged it under the bed frame. Pants and skirt
hung from the doorknob. Late at night
I padded to the closet down the hall,
grateful for a rest from unity,
past snores of old men, a Polish voice mumbling
Revelation, doors chained open in the airless heat.

We shared happiness like a piece of Scotch tape,
first on my thumb, then yours.

Pigeons in the airwell fucked
with astonished, angry moans.

In June we smelled of Hunan Wok, in July
the fan drove shadows like moods across our cheeks.

The dim avenue beyond the Windex-streaked glass
was childhood. Boys kept taking engines apart
on stoops, wiping the bolts lovingly with rags,
and the high bluish lamps flickered.

Always I returned to climb our steps
with a thudding chest, slip the key in the lock,
and come back to the present. I whispered
breathlessly, RFK was shot, Khe Sanh fell,
the Manx cat ran between two trucks . . .

We forced ourselves to betray each other:
it seemed a good use for twilight,
broken as it was by the Levolor blind.

Just to have another inch of room against the wall.

All we remembered was the red tip of the tongue,
the pupil huge in darkness, the book
held open by a ticket to a marked page.

The Bars

After work I'd go to the little bars
along the bright green river, Chloe's Lounge,
Cloverleaf, Barleycorn, it was like dying
to sit at five p.m. with a Bud so cold
it had no taste, it stung my hand,
when I returned home I missed my keys
and rang until my wife's delicate head
emerged in her high window and retreated
like a snail tucked in a luminous shell—
I couldn't find my wallet, or my paycheck,
though I drank nothing, only a few sips
that tasted like night air, a ginger ale,
nevertheless a dozen years passed, a century,
always I teetered on that high stool
while the Schlitz globe revolved so slowly,
disclosing Africa, Asia, Antarctica,
unfathomable oceans, radiant poles,
until I was a child, they would not serve me,
they handed me a red hissing balloon
but for spite I let it go, for the joy
of watching it climb past Newton Tool & Die,
for fear of cherishing it, for the pang
of watching it vanish and knowing myself
both cause and consequence.

Sonny Stitt at the Blue Coronet

His fingers don't seem to move
as he rips through secondary dominants
of "Boplicity," "Simone," "Ray's Idea."
The alto is a golden fishhook.

Why such blazing tempi when he'll die
in six weeks? Perhaps in heroin
there's a calm in which you can fit
a thousand notes into one beat.

Drums, bass, Hammond organ—
these are unnamed men, faces
you've met all your life
and bargained with, nodded to,
yet they have no difficulty
with the subtlest modulation.

The audience is three drunks,
one cursing an imaginary waitress,
one mumbling apologies, one sleeping.

Now try to eat your extremely salted cashews
so slowly there will always be one left.

Fourteen Months in the
Handbag Handle Factory

I buffed mitered staves on a grinding wheel
that threw clouds of polish in my eyes.
No one showed me how—perhaps there was no way.
I experimented with angles of pressure.
It was like sex: why didn't I know?
My ignorance renewed itself like a season.

In one grip, the template caught,
hurled back with shattering force
as if I had been making small talk
with someone who hated me—
at a close angle, almost effortless,
the bevel glittered, preternaturally smooth.

Always I spied on my hands
gliding to their assigned stations
of their own accord—to remember who I was
I held my breath a full minute.

At sunset, walled in by finished parts,
perched on a stool a stranger built,
I was a thought with the gift of death,
an insight into the tensile strength of veneer.

Once, in the corner of my eye I glimpsed
plywood from Karelia trucked in on dollies
by a crew from a rival union.
I shouted from the side of my mouth,
I'm from there, and a voice answered, *So?*

I never saw the final product,
not in the subway or the neon-lit streets—
I came to suspect a fabrication—but once
long after midnight in our stifling room
I touched her wrist and described
a rosewood-canvas tote from Macy's
and she whispered, *Yes, love.*

The Surface

The sandhogs who blasted the Battery Tunnel
jerry-rigged an escarpment a quarter mile down
but it buckled at riptide and one journeyman
was sucked into the air pocket, up through the lattice,
through the ooze under the East River, to surface
in daylight—how the hell did he remember
to drop his ninety-pound jute sack and let himself float
until a tug lowered a skiff—now no one knows his name—

Mr. Modesto, in for his second hernia, told this story
in the waiting room behind the nurses' station
at Downstate—view of a gasworks, Szechuan takeout,
cat hunting a spindled leaf, laundry on tenement roofs,
three clouds, one bright, one tinged, one darkening.

Mr. Solaris, like me an expectant father, nodded sleepily,
scratching his head and mechanically rolling the dead skin
between thumb and forefinger, perhaps to release the odor.

But Mrs. Hiram Q. Pace, whose brother had Alzheimer's,
never looked up from her sudoku, and the nameless man
in the seersucker suit with the hairline rip at one elbow,
who had never spoken since the beginning, swept up his
　　Patience
to reshuffle—how could he shuffle for himself—
so the cards hung luminous between his hands

when the nurse in the corridor cleared her throat
and we each looked up with a question on our lips
but I was the one the crooked finger summoned
to kneel by my wife and hold my breathing child.

Bridge of Voices

for Washington and Emily Roebling, after David McCullough

1

The arc is perfect in my father's mind
but he died from the rigor of his remedies
for a mangled toenail.

So I must build it.

2

J. Haigh will weave adulterated wire
into my father's ten-strand cable
and the Tenedos worm will bore a pinhole
through zinc, pitch, oakum, and tin
to riddle the pine lattice.

Let me anchor my Brooklyn foundation
fifty feet under the river bottom—
Boss Tweed will bid up the New York caisson
and scribble zeroes in the blueprint
while it is still a wall of numbers
in my father's perfect mind.

The superstructure weighs 616,640 tons
but the nib of my pen supports it
at the point where metal meets paper.

3

My husband can no longer walk or speak,
yet his quill runs across the foolscap
in equations almost too crabbed to read,
driven forward by that power, identity—

it is the war that baffled us:
14,000 dead at Antietam:
20,000 in an hour at Bull Run—

I alone can decode these squiggles
intricate as wormholes
or I believe I can, so I hear my voice
expounding tensile and centripetal force
until the contractors nod
at my sketch of a grommet.

Is it worth a single sandhog's life?

4

At eighty, I pose for my father's statue.

I suck in my breath
with the plans on my knee
and the hammer turns us into granite.

5

Now let this crucible steel
pooled in my father's Trenton mill
bear the weight of a single body.

First Night

We brought that newborn home from Maimonides
and showed her nine blue glittering streets.
Would she like the semis with hoods of snow?
The precinct? Bohack's? A lit diner?
Her eyes were huge and her gaze tilted
like milk in a pan, toward shadow.
Would she like the tenement, three dim flights,
her crib that smelled of Lemon Pledge?
We slept beside her in our long coats,
rigid with fatigue in the unmade bed.
Her breath woke us with its slight catch.
Would she approve of gray winter dawn?
We showed her daylight in our cupped hands.
Then the high clocks began booming
in this city and the next, we counted for her,
but just the strokes, not the laggards
or the tinny echoes, and we taught her
how to wait, how to watch, how to be held,
in that icy room, until our own alarm chimed.

The Living Will

I rode the subway to Gilead
where my mother lay in coma.

When we passed aboveground
I saw children playing ball
on a little diamond
in a haze of dust—

a cheerleader whirled upside down,
a bald coach placed a zero
in a grooved slot.

A home run soared into dusk
and the children froze,
but one walked away in tears.

He was talking to himself.
I tried to read his lips.

Then we entered Flatbush:
padlocked furniture stores:
in one window, a fringed lamp blazed,
in the next, an immense sofa
like a god's knees—signs
read *Sale! Sale!* but on the streets
there was no one.

At the border of Bensonhurst
a nun dragged a balky collie
on a retractable leash.

An old man in rubber sandals
lugged a sign *Repent* and argued
with the air beside him.

At Bath Beach a gap-toothed kid
waved to me from a marble stoop
and I was no longer a witness,
no longer a passerby.

I groped in my pockets
for the wadded form
with the strange stiff language
that meant *no life support.*

The North Side

I took a job at the Arnold Grill,
topping off drafts with a paddle
for the St. Johnsbury truckers.

Tuesday nights my father came in
to buy a shot of muscatel
and nurse it in a far booth
beside a small jukebox
which he plied with quarters.

He was dead so the smoke
and obscenities did not bother him.

At three a.m. I began tallying my tips—
a fortune in Canadian pennies.

Once, I confronted him:
Why do you keep coming?
Can't you rest? And why Tuesday?

He was hurt. He averted his fine eyes
and joined a conversation
about Billy Martin—

had he ruined Vida Blue?
A waitress laughed—apparently
my father knew nothing of the forkball—
and next Tuesday he did not come.

No one missed him.
The pool players cleaned the table,
rack after rack, adjusting the score
with beads on a string in midair,

the dart players paused, with pursed lips,
pushing the feathers through air
as if they had just found an opening,

but my father had not returned,
not even as a ghost, not even
as a tremor in a bettor's hand.

I locked the iron door at first light,
lowered the steel shutters,
clicked the seven padlocks,
and instead of my father,
to whom I'd spoken all my life
with bitterness, with sarcasm,

I spoke to that uncertain moment
between false dawn and dawn
when the traffic roars north,
just streaks of trapped light,
lamps go out in the charity ward,
and the tenements light up,
the highest floors first:

Why can't you rest, I said.

The Trapper Keeper

The child lost the essay she wrote
on rainfall in state capitals—
Pierre, Bismarck, Olympia—
left it on the Corona bus
and she was inconsolable
as if she forgot twilight itself.
So I set out for the Depot
past the tavern and bodega,
stockyard and shunting yard, there
where drivers relax on raffia seats
reading the gospels in Coptic or Aramaic,
and I found it: her intricate binder
green with stickers of frogs.
I slogged through triplicate forms
and lugged her homework home.
She and I were lost in fortune,
she couldn't believe her luck
or I my power, the Methodist sirens
whined very faintly, she stayed up late
writing about rainfall in Willamette,
Boise, Havre de Grace, Sioux Falls.
But I couldn't sleep for happiness,
half-wishing that dog-eared folder
had stayed safe in loss,
in the past where our steel door
with its buckling tin number
is locked like all the other tenements.

A Stoop in Bensonhurst

The deaf white alley cat
scrutinizes a firefly
skeptically, swiveling
at each lit passage.

Mystery how he survived
so long a winter.
I couldn't feed him
or drive him away.

Now he stalks the cracked cement,
all method, inventing triangles,
cornering his prey—
but what is it?

A red ant, a wisp of straw,
a shadow; or he's just testing
eye against paw.

If I call him
I won't exist—
but when my wrist turns
to write *cat*,
he's all pupil.

We almost make each other gods.
We're the self, when we die
we'll take ant and shadow.

The straw will inch ahead alone
to Spica, Deneb,
places that are just names.

1967

1

I was hired to finish interiors in Cloverdale
but I didn't know how: how to pry open
the zinc-tabbed five-gallon tub: how
to slide out the balsa paddle without leaving
a maze of white dots on oak parquet:
how deep and long to dip the bristle:
perhaps it was a problem of language: *paint*
was verb or noun or both or neither.
So I watched Mr. Colraine and Mr. Emil Toxer
but saw no common measure. Mr. Colraine
wiggled a sash brush and attacked the wall
with wide looping inward-concentric gestures
which melded as an image forms in the retina
but into blankness. Mr. Emil Toxer
knelt and inched along the molding,
crept back to his starting point, finished
five hours early, lit a Parodi, and poured himself
six ounces of Sneaky Pete from a pint stashed
in an empty stain vat. At sunset I drove home

2

through the projects, passing those small parks
where collies run canted as their Frisbees tilt,
where the swing stands at apogee and a child
spits on her hands and enters the jump rope eye
to sing herself to twilight.

3

I came to your house, dusted the narrow chime
with my cuff, realigned the two ash cans
so the crenellated one showed its best profile,
and entered your level eyes like a minnow
darting into Lake Michigan. I didn't know
how to be naked. I imagined Mr. Colraine
in his four layers of spackle-stiff mesh V-shirts
and Mr. Emil Toxer who never spilled a drop.

All I knew was: each act had a past and future,
an almost and an absolute, but the present
was just a cry, then a soft gliding return
to a dim room with a jar of Vaseline,
a votive candle, and a peony in a wineglass.

I realized almost immediately that the task
was to wait for dawn and your Manx cat
was practicing, narrowing her green stare
in anticipation of sunrise, so I followed
her light quick breaths, and here I am.

The Present

We made models: this is a moment of happiness,
this is a maple-shaded street, its yellow median line
littered with double wings: someday we might know such things
in our real lives, not just in desire.

We invented Cherryfield, Maine, nine pearl-gray Capes
with sagging porches held together by coats of gesso.
Behind the scrim of birches the Middle Branch River
glittered like the galvanized roof to a tackle shed.

We were quick and replicated a shack with a chalk sign,
CHUBBS CROAKERS SMELTS; there was barely time to read it
before it whirled into the past. And she who was driving said,
We know the coming disaster intimately but the present is
    unknowable.

Which disaster, I wondered, sexual or geological? But I was shy:
her beauty was like a language she didn't speak and had never heard.

Then we were in Holyfield and it was the hour when the child
waves from a Welcome mat, his eyes full of longing, before turning
inward to his enforced sleep. We waved back but we were gone.

The hour when two moths bump together above a pail of lures.

The hour when the Coleman lamp flickers in the screen house
above the blur of cards being shuffled and dealt amazingly fast.

All my life I have been dying, of hope and self-pity,
and an unknown force has been knitting me back together.
It happens in secret. I want to touch her and I touch her
and it registers on the glittering gauges that make the car darker
and swifter and we come to the mountains and this is all I ever
    wanted:

to enter the moth's pinhead eye, now, and never return.

Blackbird Island

Two sleepers in the pine cabin, both us,
horizon in the window like a spirit level,
Ferris Island with its single lamp, August,
annoying whoosh of the gold flies, suddenly imperceptible,
a lull covering us like a nubby cotton blanket.

Perhaps it was then I lost the skinny thread
that fastens the needles to their sticky cones,
the insouciant cloud to its ponderous shadow.
The coast was framed on her lips, but it was dusk.
I couldn't grasp how her breath held it, almost spoken.

I will never know who I am, never have a clear mind,
but moonrise will come, and the stumbling moth,
whiter in darkness, groping for the outlines of a face.

Damariscotta

1

How we loved to create a world.

Out of *gray* we made the pin-oak leaves
with their saw teeth and odd waxy sheen,
dry and matte to the touch, out of *granite*
we made the marriage house, and always
we added a flaw which we called *fire*
or *time* or *the stranger*.

2

A drop of water on the lip of a jug,
trembling, trying to hold on
for another second to the idea of sphericity—
that was us, our nakedness.

3

We worked to thwart our happiness
because it was so unexpected;
suffering tasted like our mouths.

4

We had a flagstone path, a pond, four birches,
a dog racing in tight circles, helpless
against the dream of fresh snow.

Tomorrow that red Schwinn with training wheels
must find a way to pedal itself.

5

World like a child who learned to walk
beyond our outstretched hands.

The End of Lunar Days

We were husband and wife
rowing a leaky green skiff
across the Bay of Fundy.

We faced each other,
winced at the absence
of that green stare,
and tried to focus instead
on the white Methodist steeple
or the ledger-line horizon.

How tired we were,
the insides of our knuckles ached—
the exaggerated moan of the oarlock
ceased even to annoy us.

That was the region of great tides,
so powerful their velocities
are entered on the map
like mountains or cities.

We were in love and the mind
had just begun to feast on us.

Twin shafts of light
whirled under the oar blades
and a runt bass
flickered behind the rudder
with a wisp of spent line
dangling from its chops.

Which of us was crying?
Would we ever know?

Did we point out the great clouds
that have no identity
and the pitiful afternoon stars
with their portentous tentative names—
Aldebaran, Spica?

"The Summer Triangle,"
one said to the other,
and the echo returned
solemn with deep water
from the granite cliffs.

We would deceive each other
to explain the ache of estrangement,
we would abandon ourselves
to make sense of that loneliness,
and then what?

A corkscrew of distant gulls wheeling,
calling, and the mind among them,
calling a little louder.

Could our voices reach the child
doing cartwheels on the jetty,
frantically as he grew tiny,
and then turning away,
and the Airedale turning also,
you swore it half-shrugged—

a door closed in Canada,
a red balloon rose into that vastness,
for a moment we saw the string,

then we lost it,
we hoarded it in our minds—
we whispered to no one,
to the frayed horizon, *string*.

Beauty

Wielding blue Sheffield shears
and foxed by a night of anti-love
I squint to clip the old man's hair
though he has so little—
    how gracefully it falls
(like Wile E. Coyote stepping
off a cliff), holding its greasy curl
in midair as on terrazzo tile.

This customer just wants to tell me
once more how his wife left him
on the steamer to Salonika
early in the Ford administration,
though now it's the boat in his story
that cuts a wake like a white scar.

The Rain-streaked Avenues of Central Queens

It ends badly, this glass of wine,
before you drink it
you have to drink a prior glass,
before you sip you gulp,
before you chug the bottle
you pour it down your throat,
before we lie together
naked, we divorce, before we rest
we grow old, it ends in chaos,
   but it is delicious,
when we wake it is the past,
we are the faces staring
from the high lit window,
the unmet lovers, the rivals
who do not exist,
united in a radiance
that will not fade at dawn.

The Next Apartment

I lived beside the lovers on that linden-shaded industrial block
between Linwood and Crescent. How they argued! Once
he pounded his head against the lintel in a rain of plaster.
Once I watched her walk into the rain carrying her Lhasa Apso,
step into a cab, and give the finger to their lit window.

They fought with themselves when the other was gone,
struggling so hard with each word: *I, you, tomorrow.*
Since they loved each other forever, seconds were lethal,
split seconds tormented them like the strange bluebottle flies
that zoomed from buried drums under Ebbets Field.

How they reconciled, bearing each other elaborate gifts:
silk orchid, glass horse, a necklace that flickered like flame.
They paced on the landing, practicing complex apologies
that turned seamlessly to justifications—how helpless
they were against being right! When they saw me

in the stairwell, they were relieved:
someone sane, a human, someone who will die.
And they explained: *Sorry about yesterday, sorry
about tomorrow . . .* they had a ferocious need
to be remembered, since they were going
alone into time itself. I wanted to ask them,
*Do you think we can create a void in a supercollider
and destroy not just the world but the night sky?*

But I had no inkling what the self is,
or loneliness, or marriage, or the universe
sealed in zeroes like honey in a comb.

So instead we talked about the Mets, Gooden's arm
going stale, Strawberry losing that amazing insight
that can pick up the seam on a rotating curveball.

And they turned the key in their lock: male, female,
it made no difference, they were the same person,
and entered their tiny room, and I entered sleep.

Freedom and Chance

She says, There is another city, exactly like this:
same sardonic cat, complacent dog, fat-chested sparrow
trilling its brains out before daybreak, identical abandon
and thrilling sorrow, familiar machinery chuffing
in darkness—belt sander, leaf blower, radial arm saw.
But that world is Ditmas Park, this is Dyker Heights.
The law is like wind; it has no self.
There Frank Viola stars, here Julio Franco.
Here light is a wave, there a particle.
Here we marry and play cribbage in a tiny house
with a porch swing and complicated locks.
There, you plod through deserted chain stores
in search of someone you cannot know. Here
the names of God, blurted from passing cars.
There, the milk truck and its loud crate of empties.

Twilight in Canarsie

In these long slant-lit streets, she says,
you will find factories that once made shoehorns,
waffle irons, or pearl cuff links, and storefront churches
where voices adored the Living God while tambourines
clashed a little behind the beat, and Jiffy Lubes,
and beauty parlors where bored calico cats
licked their paws disdainfully, perhaps a movie house
with posters of Garbo and a marquee with detachable vowels,
a candy store selling egg cremes and roped red licorice,
a little bar with a jar of pig trotters and a lone fly
stumbling in and out of a shaft of daylight, a library
reeking of mucilage, a funeral home with bas-relief columns,
a shoe repairman listening to scores from Chicago,
the tenement where we made love and each thrust
carried us deeper into the past, as if we were an engine
careening back to childhood, then the shunting yard,
the park with its whirling jump rope, the red brick school
that manufactured absolutes, Sphere, Pyramid, Dodecahedron,
while children tried to carve their names clear through their desks,
the cemetery of lovers immobilized by marble wings—

why is it always twilight when we die, she asks,
and Canarsie where we are born again?

The Long Marriage

1

I love my life, she says,
but really I would like to be elsewhere.
I love the pull of the dog's leash
and the air between us when we sleep.

I am amazed how decisions
are made in dreams, with an absent mind,
and last forever. I just like elsewhere better.
I would take you with me if I could.

2

It is snowing, as always in that window,
and the old dog, gray-muzzled,
listens with his head on his paws,
breathing hard in sleep.

A Night in Brooklyn

We undid a button,
turned out the light,
and in that narrow bed
we built the great city—
water towers, cisterns,
hot asphalt roofs, parks,
septic tanks, arterial roads,
Canarsie, the intricate channels,
the seacoast, underwater mountains,
bluffs, islands, the next continent,
using only the palms of our hands
and the tips of our tongues, next
we made darkness itself, by then
it was time for daybreak
and we closed our eyes
until the sun rose
and we had to take it all to pieces
for there could be only one Brooklyn.

PART TWO

Elsewhere

The Long Struggle Against the Mind

It colored the oak: we unpinned the leaves.
It invented the wind: a bowing, a resistance,
a pressure, a rolling without an eye.
We undid that labor: there was no wind,
the wind was in the mind. It made us undress,
stand face-to-face flushed as if in front
of a shy sorrowful mirror. It made us
resist it, try to discover something hard
and soft besides hardness and softness,
a world, a room with a blue blue curtain,
a small bottomless sky, a dog dish, a wineglass
with a hairline crack, Evora, a wife,
a husband: then it unmade us: we were elms
with zippers, who knew they would die,
we were clouds who had no choice
but to advance naked in mind-breaking silence
toward that shining absent presence.

Evora

Maybe we can talk our way out of death
given that it disappears so disingenuously
whenever you look for it, so do we,
leaving only the track of a snail
in the stucco alcove where we catnapped
in Evora, in late summer, scrunched
in the osier bed, before you knew me,
before I didn't know you, when the future ended,
cracked sun in the mirror, when the finches
instructed us in thin scattered voices
to stand our ground against delight.

Notes from the Foothills

The male fly lives sixteen days. The female, twenty-four.
The hatchling never grows: slips out full-size and zooms.

Rain in the orchards. The crests of the Dolomites are smudgy.
Logy wind probes the cinched curtain.
She murmurs a name in sleep. The fly zips away.

Once I tried to kill it. Once I succeeded.
I had to scrape wings from the lines of my palm.
They never lost transparency. Mostly I failed.
It took off backwards, five times faster than my hand.

I formed a picture in my mind and tried to destroy it.
Would it have been easier without that image?

The fly has wing stubs, halteres, attached directly to its eyes,
bypassing the mind: the wings are wired to body hairs.

Nine stormy nights. Nothing can stop the Airedale
from stiffening his body into an S-shape, staring incredulously,
and shitting in the lupines, nothing stops the eggs from opening.

In each eye, four thousand lenses, in each lens
a different I, a pattern of diffracted sparks
that equals two middle-aged lovers and a judgmental cat.

A bee in its career makes a quarter teaspoon of honey.
A fly makes nothing. It will eat our bodies
though it is mouthless, just a sponge and sticker.

When it dies, Altair dies, trapped tonight behind cloud cover,
Andromeda, and Betelgeuse, still below the northern horizon.

This village lives off plums, walnuts, and black wine.
Volley of slate roofs. Back country of stone walls.
Mills on swift rivers. Yards glinting with chestnuts.

Was it you who invented death, blank page?

Mid-August in the Dolomites

We communicated by cheeses,
unwrapping them gingerly,
parting the crust with a fork,
tasting dew, must, salt,
raising an eyebrow,

or we let Chianti talk for us,
rolling it in the glass,
staring—it was sleek and shiny
as the pupil, and stared back—
or we undressed each other;

we took long walks hand in hand
in the vineyards, the pastures,
resenting each other bitterly
for our happiness that excluded us
as surely as the world did,
mountain after mountain.

The Simulacra

They were driving into the mountains, helplessly married,
sometimes touching each other's cheek with a fingernail
gingerly: the radio played ecstatic static: certain roads
marked with blue enamel numbers led to cloud banks,
or basalt screes, or dim hotels with padlocked verandas.
Sometimes they quarreled, sometimes they grew old,
the wind was constant in their eyes, it was their own breeze,
they made it. Small towns flew past, Rodez, Cahors,
limestone quarries, pear orchards, children racing
after hoops, wobbling when their shadows wavered,
infants crying for fine rain, old women on stoops
darning gray veils—and who were we, watching?
Doubles, ghosts, the ones who would tell of the field
where they pulled over, bluish tinge of the elms, steepness
of the other's eyes, glowworm hidden in its glint,
how the rain was dusk and now is darkness.

A Night in Cáceres

We gave each other the absolute gift.
And we were scared.
We wanted to take it back.
We didn't know how to mention it:
we hardly knew our own names.
Give me that night back.
That fly fumbling in the webs.
That touch, like moonlight on your arm,
but free, not determined by the laws
of distance and falling bodies.
A thrush chirring after midnight
with great confidence and brokenness.
The hush of the Tajo River
as it pools towards Navas.
We listened for the other's breath.
Sometimes we heard it, sometimes rain.
We slept in the crook of the arm.
At first light we flinched.
There was no other. No such gift.
In the mirror, just a high cloud
and Venus, brighter in daylight.

Andalusian *Coplas* and Song Fragments

Versions of anonymous originals

1

Jesus, I'm dying,
rid me of this man
who reeks of husband
all night long.

2

To play my guitar
for the dark girl
I washed my hands with mint.

3

Face-to-face,
nothing to say—
we're like Valencia
circled by walls.

4

To forget you
I'd need another sun,
another moon, commandments
from another God.

5

Body full of poems
like a hornet's nest—
each pushing the next
to see which comes out first.

6

Go ask your mother
to put you in an alcove
and light candles in front of you.
Tell her I'm done with you.

7

Run and tell your mom
to shear and fleece you—
let her give you suck again
and teach you to be a man.

8

Don't say you loved me,
say you loved a stone
that sank in the ocean.

9

Get out, fuck you,
you're like a lamp in a toilet,
you shine on anything.

10

Darling, when you're with strangers,
don't do that little thing
you did for me.

11

Anyone who can sing
with a grievance like mine
better have bristles
around his heart.

12

Because I'm a stranger
I ask the locals,
Who is that dark girl
who looks so good in mourning?

13

Love you? Definitely.
Talk to you? Whenever possible.
Marry you? The fig
won't fall from that tree.

14

That idiot girl thought I'd cry.
Doesn't she know the taverns
sell little portions of happiness?

15

When your messenger arrived
bearing the news
that you no longer love me,
even my cat chuckled.

16

I knocked three times
at midnight on your iron gate.
For someone dying of love, little girl,
you're a heavy sleeper.

17

Your eyes and mine tangled
like blackberry vines
under the owner's fence.

18

Some quarrels are whims.
Some quarrels are illusions.
Some quarrels you move into
like a rented room.

19

If I had five fingers,
I'd give one not to have met you.

I'd give my fourth finger
not to know your name.

I'd give my third
not to have touched you.

I'd give my second
not to have made love.

Christ, if I had only one finger,
I'd give it up happily
never to have seen your face,

firefly of the morning.

20

A poor man stinks of death.
Throw him in the pit.
Jingle in your pocket?
Requiescat in pace. Amen.

Eight Spanish Riddles

Versions of anonymous originals

1

I'm a terrible guest,
nobody wants me,
but you can't remember me
unless you entertain me—
who am I?
Hunger.

2

Green, all green,
green birth, and now
I sit on top of God?
The crown of thorns.

3

Little plate of hazelnuts,
on the shelf by day,
spilt at night?
The stars.

4

What did the shepherd
see in the mountains
that the king can't see,
the pope on his throne won't see,
God Almighty shall never see?
His equal.

5

I was quiet in my room
when they came for me.
I'm still a prisoner, but my house
escaped through the windows—
who am I?
Fish in a net.

6

I walked down a road that didn't come back
and they took off the cape that I never wore.
I went to a lettuce patch and picked apples.
The owner of the chestnuts arrived.
—What are you doing in my lettuce patch?
—I'm gathering acorns
sweet as artichoke honey.
What am I?
A lame riddle.

7

I strut in the barnyard,
pecking at chaff.
What am I?
The hen.
—Shit on people
who think they know everything.
—Since I guessed your riddle,
I shit in your mouth.

8

Five oxen plowing
with a single harrow—
what dark work is this
in a fallow field?
The hand writing.

Old French Riddles

Versions of anonymous originals

What never was and never shall be?
—*Mouse nest in cat's ear.*

Passes through these woods and leaves no shadow?
—*Tolling bell.*

Dead and still dances?
—*Winter oak leaf.*

Sings going down, cries coming up?
—*Bucket in the well.*

Frayed, unraveling,
but the needle never passed here?
—*A cloudy sky.*

Flounce, flicker,
red rose in midair?
—*A man walking with a lantern.*

Four little thighs in bed
with a zigzag in the middle?
—*Walnut.*

Round as a ducat,
faster than a horseman?
—*The eye.*

Devoured us and we didn't notice?
—*Time.*

PART THREE

No Time

There Is No Time, *She Writes*

We have to bomb the rebel cities
from a great height, find shelter
for the refugees, carry a sick kitten
to the shade of a blighted elm,
fall in love, walk by the breakwater,
learn the words to separate,
marry, see a lawyer, negotiate,

and always the wind seethes
in the bladelike leaves,
always the ant under its burden,
proud and indomitable, *she writes*,
always the faint music, the touch
of the other's hand, and no way
to return, or even turn,
no way to face ourselves:

writing this, I pressed so hard,
she says, the words are embedded
in the grain of the desk
and it is dark but I sense you
listening, trying to frame an answer
there where the dark turns inward
and a small bell chimes
in the stupefying heat.

The Lake Behind the Branches

The suicides were walking sideways
on their half-lit screened porch
cradling brimful mint juleps
and frowning—*must not spill.*
One tiny umbrella was soaked.
It was almost evening, the pale crests
of the pines seemed long ago.
Had they killed themselves for sexual peace?
Because the mountain ash kept wavering?
I would have asked them, but all that summer
I felt like someone who just woke—
in a moment everything will be obvious:
the meaning of the faces, the shadow craning
behind their backs like a scrupulous tutor,
the faint clear bell that must come
from across deep water, from an island
or a ship. Anika, since I am not dead,
I can't stop counting, though the sum
is just nightfall, nakedness, the fat bee
zooming freely through the golden wisps.

The Island in Autumn

In the novel there was a blue house by a lake
and two lovers sat on a porch wrapped in blankets.
The plot was how slowly the clouds passed,
how hard it was to get from one second to the next,
how each moment had a little rind, like a seed,
you had to scratch at it, but by the time you finished
you were in the next day, the next era in fact—

the lovers were reading short stories
in which they came to know each other,
the setting was Navas, they rarely spoke,
but from the island, music reached them—
the depth of the water made the chords very precise
though played haltingly—and laughter,
laughter of children, that contains threats, tears,
amazement and abdication, and the crackle

of a loud pine fire: also commands to a dog,
sit, fetch, roll over, drop it, calm down, be good,
and the dog found its way into the stories,
sniffed the tall red oaks there, delighted
at scaring the shy arrogant mourning doves,
drank noisily from the brook, then looked
for a master, but the novel closed
just when the motive of the clouds was most secret.

The PowerPoint

That century passed in spurts. All our responses—rage, shame—
were etched on our foreheads with a steel-nib Bic.
Yet we could not feel them. Barely remember their names.
Between the plenary and keynote we aged a dozen years.
During the breakout sessions we gained back a few breaths,
a moment of regained clarity when we spoke of Kara melting
and allowed ourselves to choke with passion. Passion
we could not feel. That hall swam with soft glints
reflected off watch crystals, iPhones, chandeliers,
racing screens that cannot move. Always the PowerPoint
advanced from whale to dolphin to pollack to krill.
The image clicked forward like days, frame to frame,
though we longed to know what happens in between.
The voice followed sinuously. It cannot stop.
How we missed the blue chalk dust of our apprenticeship,
our yellow dog-eared legal pads crawling with statistics
inscribed by hand, poison in Jacmel, Bhopal, Battambang.
The numbers themselves had grown bland, oddly distanced
from the marlite on which they were projected.
Yet we were children a second ago, eager to learn
to inscribe the great zero, our mouths open,
teaching ourselves to spell, tell time, and tie our shoes,
sailor knot, scout knot, as if your love could stop us
drawing those knots tighter and tighter in the mind.

Psalm to Be Read with Closed Eyes

Ignorance will carry me through the last days,
the blistering cities, over briny rivers
swarming with jellyfish, as once my father
carried me from the car up the narrow steps
to the white bed, and if I woke, I never knew it.

Summertime

When we tried to blast free of earth's pull,
whirling debris hammered us in near space—
a toaster, a blender, spare parts to satellites,
Father's putting iron, Baby's bronze shoe—
we had to turn back with a breached hull
and touch down on the charred launch pad
where the brass band that had plodded to see us off
welcomed us with sardonic oompahs: no Mars,
no Venus, no moons of Jupiter: we would grow old
to "Summertime" on a dented tuba, self-hating trumpet,
trombone uncoiling like a mantis, each reprise
the last, in the flickering light of storms.

Time

To change your mind, I made a perfect replica of the coast—
vase-crested elms, birches sloughing their papery bark,
self-contained poplars, slow-whirling maple keys.
I sketched in our marriage bed, unmoving ceiling fan,
the mirror withheld and pollen-dusted like lake water.
I had forgotten the high, almost motionless clouds,
clouds of early summer, with their insidious shadow
lighting like a fly on the rim of a wineglass.
The rain like a cat behind the rosebushes. The reprieve.
Novice fireflies, here and not here, here-and-not-here.
Strawberry starts that grow so wild, woody clumps,
without the touch of a hand. Instead of time,
I inked in suffering. I meant it to be mine,
but because I couldn't feel, I pressed too hard—
through the rip I saw darkness, your eyes,
emptiness of a room, night with its billion lights.

The Past

1

I was arguing with you. I was eager to prove
you were cruel and I was kind. You parried every word,
every thought. It was almost autumn. A great fatigue
passed like cloud shadow over crinkled pin-oak leaves.
It occurred to me: what if I succeeded?
Your margin of maneuver would be infinite,
and I constricted to suffering: this was your nature:
to trump me, like sleep in a dream—but it was too late
to take my words back, dusk had fallen and the blue moth,
tentative as breath, tried to steer a path around it.

2

Now it is night I have to convince you it is dark.
I gather pieces of night and show them to you
but you just shake your head: an old man's cupped hands.
I try to show you night, in the screen, the mirror,
a cat's-eye marble, the blank page. Night
hardening around the porch lamp like an impenetrable shield.
No, no. I try to show you *no*, the shape of your lips,
but I am too good at this now, I am locked in my version,
it opens into the infinite past, an old man wagging his finger.
I am lying beside you with closed eyes, it is morning,
you have just left, the doorway smells of mown grass.

Three Twilights

1

Before I was born, I didn't exist, no obstacle,
no trick question, just a half-lit tenement, a narrow street
curling on itself like a cat's tail, a child on a porch
bouncing a ball, frowning, sticking out her tongue,
a sparrow pecking dust, and the voices building their case,
telling how I would suffer, why, what I could expect in return,
lisping a little, repeating themselves but incurably persuasive,
the child keeping score doggedly, backtracking at each new zero,
the ball flattening a hair, returning to the cupped hand.

2

We adored each other but kept getting caught in the description:
couple at evening, trembling, a name like a balky zipper.

3

When I was dead and had no hope, I lay among dry looped weeds
still silky at their bent tips, to watch the flat-bottomed cumulus
inching toward Gilead, two flies rubbing their legs together
with a furious gentleness, dusk, and the mind observing:
a last voice droned on in the gloating accent of suffering:
whatever force might free me, it was not the will or the night sky.

Return to the Capital

They imagined they would sleep together,
then they slept together—
they thought to rest afterwards,
arm in arm, listening to rain,
so they rested, but it snowed,
they woke in silence
(the silence woke them),
they had not imagined the pain
of dressing, sorting clothes
back into male and female—
in the mirror, instead of a face,
they saw two reflections:

if this is happiness,
how shall we leave it,
if this is grief, how to enter it,
if this is just a rented room,
where are the doors, the stairs,
the streets, the endless city.

Acknowledgments

Thanks to the editors of the magazines in which the following poems were published:

The American Poetry Review: "Waking in Greenpoint in Late August," "Central Brooklyn," "Making Shelves," "The Long Marriage," "The Dead Reveal Secrets of Brooklyn."

The Atlantic: "Summertime."

NYCBigCityLit.com: "The Living Will."

The Cortland Review: "Old French Riddles," "Sonny Stitt at the Blue Coronet."

Drunken Boat: "Letter from Home."

Field: "The Long Struggle Against The Mind," "Evora," "Blackbird Island," "Notes from the Foothills." ("Evora" also appeared in *Poetry Daily*.)

Hanging Loose: "Furnished Room on Pearl Street," "Twilight in Canarsie," "The Trapper Keeper."

Harvard Review: "Red Antares in a Blue Mirror."

The Kenyon Review: "The Present."

The Literary Review: "Andalusian *Coplas* and Song Fragments," numbers 1, 2, 3, 4, 5, 6, 7, 8, and 12 (translations).

The Manhattan Review: "Return to the Capital" (published under the title "A Night in the Capital"), "A Night in Cáceres," "The End of Lunar Days," "Bridge of Voices," "Fourteen Months in the Handbag Handle Factory," "Flatlands."

The New Republic: "Time," "Freedom and Chance."

The New Yorker: "Damariscotta" (published under the title "Newfane"), "There Is No Time, *She Writes*," "The Bars."

Ploughshares: "1967," "The Surface."

Poetry: "The Simulacra," "Mid-August in the Dolomites" (published under the title "Engagement in the Dolomites"), "The Dead Remember Brooklyn," "A Night in Brooklyn," "The Rain-streaked Avenues of Central Queens," "Psalm to Be Read with Closed Eyes."

Poetry London: "The Island in Autumn."

Swink: "A Stoop in Bensonhurst" (published under the title "A Stoop in South Brooklyn").

The Threepenny Review: "The North Side," "The Past," "The PowerPoint."

Tin House: "Eight Spanish Riddles," "The Lake Behind the Branches."

Upstreet: "Beauty," "Three Twilights."

West Branch: "Andalusian *Coplas* and Song Fragments," numbers 11, 14, 15, 16, 18, 19, and 20; "The Next Apartment." ("The Next Apartment" also appeared in *Poetry Daily.*)

I'm grateful to the MacDowell Colony, the Virginia Center for the Creative Arts, and the Corporation of Yaddo, and to the John Simon Guggenheim Memorial Foundation and the American Academy of Arts and Letters, for support that helped me write this book.

Thanks also to Deborah Garrison, my editor, to Caroline Zancan, and to Philip Fried.

A NOTE ABOUT THE AUTHOR

D. Nurkse is the author of nine previous books of poetry. His work has received awards from the American Academy of Arts and Letters, the John Simon Guggenheim Memorial Foundation, the National Endowment for the Arts, and the Whiting Foundation. He has also written widely on human rights. A former poet laureate of Brooklyn, he lives in that borough.

A NOTE ON THE TYPE

The text type in this book was set in Jenson, a font designed for the Adobe Corporation by Robert Slimbach in 1995. Jenson is an interpretation of the famous Venetian type cut in 1469 by the Frenchman Nicolas Jenson (c. 1420–1480).

Composed by North Market Street Graphics, Lancaster, Pennsylvania

Printed and bound by Thomson-Shore, Dexter, Michigan

Book design by Robert C. Olsson